A KID'S GUIDE TO

# Philadelphia

Photography by Paul Scharff

Written by Ellen W. Leroe

First published in the United States
of America by:

Twin Lights Publishers, Inc.
8 Hale Street
Rockport, Massachusetts 01966
Telephone: (978) 546-7398
http://www.twinlightspub.com

ISBN: 978-1-934907-06-1
ISBN: 1-934907-06-5

10 9 8 7 6 5 4 3 2 1

Book design by
SYP Design & Production, Inc.
http://www.sypdesign.com

Printed in China

"Are we there yet?" Yes, you are, if that means Philly! Whether you live here, are planning to visit, or just want to explore from the comfort of your home, *A Kid's Guide to Philadelphia* is a spirited journey through America's "birthplace of independence."

Kids of all ages, preschool through young teens, will love this fun and fact-filled guidebook that offers a sneaky peek at stuff that no one ever shows or tells you: Who put a "Billy Penn Curse" on all Philly pro sports? What's the "Whiz wit" secret when ordering a Philly cheesesteak?

*A Kid's Guide to Philadelphia* uses a dictionary format to showcase sizzling sites and awesome attractions from A to Z, brought vividly to life in Paul Scharff's eye-popping color photographs. This softcover gem isn't a snooze cruise of boring facts, but a shake-you-wide-awake blast of nonstop adventures and activities. Kids will find out where to see a fire-breathing bronze dragon, and an alien being from outer space that's made from steel. They'll learn where to meet 30 of the biggest, baddest—and boniest—dinos, dive deep in a real World War II submarine, or slide down the jumbo-sized Phanatic Shoe at the Phillies' ball park.

Philadelphia offers something for every kid's interest, whether it's major league sports, medicine, architecture, or world-class music or dance. The city's rich array of historical sites extends as far back as 1700, and this book is packed with fascinating facts and photos of its proud past, as well as its phenomenal present. Just ask Ben Franklin, George Washington, William Penn, or Betsy Ross. *A Kid's Guide to Philadelphia* brings the Founding Fathers (and Mother!) to life with stories and tie-ins to their homes, and places associated with their accomplishments.

The following pages offer a head-spinning number of attractions, from the Underground Railroad stop at the Johnson House, to the huge collection of black dolls at the Philadelphia Doll Museum, to the Liberty Bell. And don't forget the rockin' buildings, open air spaces and parks, fountains, and beyond-incredible things to see and do for free. The colorful pictures, paired with writer Ellen W. Leroe's playful, informative text, make for a perfect souvenir that can be read and enjoyed over and over again. Kids, grownups, and readers of all ages will want to jump onboard this rollicking tour bus of a book, and giggle at, point to, and admire all the sensational stops along the way of this unforgettable Philadelphia adventure.

## Academy of Natural Sciences
### It's Dino-Mite!

Put on your excavating gear and hunt for real fossils at the Academy of Natural Science's *Big Dig*. Meet up with the skeletons of T. rex and 29 of the other big, bad Brontosaurus boys inside *Dinosaur Hall*. Skip through the tropical rain-forest setting of *Butterflies* where hundreds of exotic, winged creatures soar overhead, or crawl through a log, investigate a real beehive, and touch a legless lizard in *Outside-In*.

There's so much to see and do at the Academy you better come early. Use your CityPASS or Philadelphia Pass for almost half the price of admission.

## Adventure Aquarium
### Swim with the Hippos?

Sure, and walk past teeth-baring crocodiles, as well! At the 200,000-square-foot Adventure Aquarium in Camden, kids can see hippos, manatees, crocs, 20 species of African birds, and thousands of colorful, exotic fish. The aquarium offers all that in their *West African River Experience*, plus a 40-foot-long underwater tunnel teeming with huge sharks. If that doesn't satisfy all your wishes for fishes, how about five hands-on "TOUCH" exhibits that include jellyfish, stingrays, and *more* sharks?

### Arden Theatre
### Drama-rama!

Founded in 1988, the Arden Theatre prides itself on bringing to life the most exciting stories from books, music, poetry, and nonfiction. You can watch children's theater all year long, enjoying productions like *Peter Pan* or *If You Give a Mouse a Cookie*.

The Arden Kids' Crew offers classes so you can learn how to put on shows yourself! The theatre is at 40 North 2nd Street, and kids get in for half price.

### Art Museum of Philadelphia

*Fantabulous.* How better to describe the city's "Museum on the Hill?" The Philadelphia Museum of Art was built in 1928 to look like a Greek temple, only grander. There are incredible collections of art, as well as *entire* rooms and buildings in there, too. There's a Chinese Palace Hall, a 12th-century French cloister, and a 16th-century Indian temple hall, among others. Daily American Art Kids Tours, family workshops, and kids' programs are on Sunday afternoons. Sundays are always pay-what-you-can for admission.

### Awbury Arboretum
### Geez, Trees!

The Awbury Arboretum in Germantown is bursting with English-style gardens, trails, ponds, and flowers. Kids can explore specially-themed gardens, like the *Candy, Pizza*, and *Rainbow Carrot Gardens*, or learn all about animals, insects, trees, and farming offered in the Summer Nature Program. There is no admission to tour the grounds and it's open all day year round.

## Ballet, Pennsylvania
## Tutu Wonderful!

What's more beautiful than watching ballerinas in costume gliding across a stage? You can enjoy fantastic dancing by the Pennsylvania Ballet at the Academy of Music opera house. The troop has forty dancers and puts on six productions a year, including the magical *Nutcracker*.

## Bartram's Garden
## Petal Power

This historic garden along the Schuylkill River was first owned by royal botanist, John Bartram. It's America's oldest surviving botanical garden. The site has loads of flowering shrubs and trees, five active beehives, and the 1728 farmhouse offers tours and cool exhibits of North American objects and tools dating back 3,000 years! Admission is $5 for the farmhouse tour, and gardens and grounds are free.

## Ben Franklin
## Amazing Founding Father

Inventor, statesman, writer and printer, Benjamin Franklin did it all. The man of many talents was born in Boston in 1706, and moved to Philadelphia at the age of 17. Called America's colonial celebrity, Philly's Founding Father came up with a number of firsts: zoo; library; postal service; and fire company. He invented bifocals, swim fins, the lightning rod, the Franklin Stove, and the glass armonica, to name a few. People think of him as the spirit of this great city. Can you find where this statue of him is located in the city? Find the Answer on page 45.

### Benjamin Franklin Bridge
### Twinkle Twinkle

This 9,650-foot-long suspension bridge started out as the Delaware River Port Authority Bridge in 1926, but it was renamed in 1956 for Ben Franklin. It connects Philadelphia and Camden, New Jersey, and was the longest suspension bridge in the world. Others are now longer, but few are quite as magical looking at night.

### Benjamin Franklin Parkway
### "Slice of Paris"

What's one mile long, runs through the heart of Philadelphia's finest museums, sculptures, fountains, and parks, and was designed to look like a beautiful wide boulevard in Paris? It's the Ben Franklin Parkway! The Parkway is a perfect place for parades, especially with the 109 flags of different countries lining both sides.

### Betsy Ross House
### A 13-Star Experience

Did Betsy Ross really sew our first flag, the Stars and Stripes? Did she actually live in this historic little brick house that was built around 1740? There's a lot about Elizabeth Griscom Ross Ashburn Claypoole—yup, that's her full name—that remains a mystery. However, it's still a great experience to visit the Betsy Ross House and discover how people lived in Colonial Philadelphia. On Sundays, Betsy talks history and reads children's stories.

### Blue Signs
### Takes the Mystery Out of History

Quick, how good are you at spotting these Blue Signs? The Pennsylvania Historical and Museum Commission post these historical markers to tell the story of people and events in Philadelphia. They have a blue background with gold lettering to honor the state's official colors. How many of these blue signs are posted in the city? They're more than you think! You'll have to look at the Answer on page 45 to find out.

MERIWETHER LEWIS
(1774-1809)
With William Clark he led the transcontinental Lewis & Clark Expedition, 1803-1806. Lewis prepared for the journey & later deposited its significant specimens, journals, and other artifacts here in Philadelphia.

PENNSYLVANIA HISTORICAL AND MUSEUM COMMISSION, 2003

### Board Game Art Park
### Your Move!

If you've ever imagined playing with giant checkers, dominoes, or chess pieces, then the Municipal Services Building is the place to find them. Artists Daniel Martinez, Renee Petropoulos, and Roger White worked together to create this way cool *Your Move* sculpture. The jumbo-sized Monopoly, checkers, Parcheesi, and domino pieces sit on the squares of Thomas Paine Plaza like a game board. But don't try picking one up. They're bolted down!

## Boathouse Row
### Rowing Front and Center

These fifteen Gothic and Late Victorian buildings are located on the east bank of the Schuylkill River and are considered the center of the rowing community around the U.S. They're home to social and rowing clubs and even the Schuylkill Navy! The boathouses are lit up at night, changing colors for different occasions. What a sparkling, spectacular sight!

## Bourse Building
### Shop Away!

Bourse means a place of exchange, and this old business center began in 1895 as the first commodities exchange in the country. It was also one of the first steel-framed buildings to be constructed. The grain dealers, export agents, and Commercial and Maritime Exchanges are long gone, but you can now shop at souvenir stores, dine in the large food court, or take in a movie at this historic, busy center.

### Campo's & Cheesesteak Whiz Wit

One of Philadelphia's best-known and yummiest treats is the cheesesteak. This is how to make this awesome sandwich: fill a big hoagie roll with thin sliced strips of beef round, grilled over a bed of onions. For the full effect, order your sandwich "Whiz wit" like Philly experts, meaning hefty helpings of Cheez Wiz and fried onions. Try one yourself at Campo's Deli on Market Street. (A local fancy restaurant in Philadelphia sells a super cheesesteak sandwich for $100!)

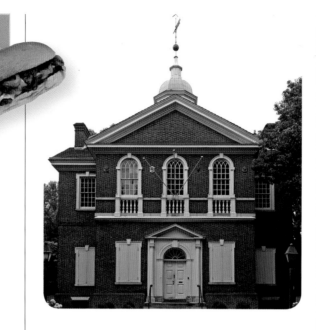

### Carpenters' Hall
### Lots of History

This building is full of history! Ben Franklin opened the first lending library in America here and it is where famous people like Paul Revere, George Washington, Samuel Adams, and John Adams once stood. The east side of the main room is where a group of representatives from 12 of the 13 colonies met as the First Continental Congress. These men worked hard to try to settle their grievances with England during the early years of the American Revolution. Visit the museum and learn why this building was built; when it was used as a hospital, and what happened when it was a bank.

### Children's Hospital of Philadelphia

When started in 1855, this was the very first children's hospital in the world. At that time, many children under the age of 12 were dying from smallpox, typhoid, and scarlet fever. The hospital offered free care and medicine, saw a total of 373 young patients the first year, and held just twelve beds. Today, the Children's Hospital of Philadelphia is ranked as the best children's hospital in the U.S.

### Chinatown

Philadelphia's Chinatown area is made up of just six city blocks. But its Friendship Gate makes this Chinese community special. The colorful arch is one of the largest authentic Chinese gates outside of China. Built in 1982 by artists from China, see how many birds and dragons you can find. While you're here, pop into one of the red-and-green pagoda-style phone booths, munch a fortune cookie, or enjoy great meals at over 50 restaurants.

## Citizens Bank Park
## Grand Slam Fun

The stadium of the Phillies baseball team was built in 2004, with 43,000 seats and knockout views. Each time someone hits a homer, the outlined Liberty Bell in right center field lights up, swings, and rings! You can climb and play games in the Phanatic Phun Zone, build your own miniature Phanatic mascot, or slide down the insides of a monster Phanatic Shoe. If that makes you hungry, head on over to the Phood Stand for kid-sized meals, one dollar hot dogs, pretzels, and other treats.

## Christ Church Burial Ground
## Hallowed Ground

Christ Church was built as a simple wooden building in 1695 and is called the "Nation's Church." William Penn was baptized here, and brass plaques mark the pews of George and Martha Washington, John and Abigail Adams, Betsy Ross, and others. Many notable historic figures are buried in the church's burial ground a few streets away. Can you find five of the signers of the Declaration of Independence who are buried here? Find who they are on page 45.

## City Hall
### Big Wedding Cake!

Philadelphia City Hall is the largest masonry building in the world, as well as the tallest at 511 feet. The cast-iron statue of William Penn on top is the biggest single piece of sculpture in the world! It took 30 years to build this "Victorian wedding cake of Renaissance style" (1871-1900), and it's famous as the geographic center of the city. Take the small elevator on the seventh floor to the observation deck tower for an awesome view that stretches for 30 miles!

## City of Brotherly Love
## Sisterly, too!

Philadelphia is known as the "City of Brotherly Love." It's more than a nickname, though. It comes from the translation of two Greek words. *Philos* means love, and *adelphos* means brother. William Penn called his Pennsylvania colony Philadelphia because he wanted people of all faiths and colors to worship freely, and care for each other.

## City Tavern
## Kids & Families Welcome

The original inn was built in 1773, and one year later Paul Revere rode up to the City Tavern to announce the closing of the port of Boston by the British. The Tavern became the meeting place for the delegates of the First and Second Continental Congresses and other politically involved citizens. Inside, enjoy recipes from Martha Washington and Thomas Jefferson, or try the Founding Father Special, and if you're lucky you just might spot Ben Franklin on a bench outside.

## CityPASS, Philadelphia
## Don's *Pass* it Up!

Want to be the star in your family? Then tell them about the Philadelphia CityPASS. It lets you go to the city's top attractions like the Franklin Institute, the Philadelphia Zoo, and the National Constitution Center for one low price. You can pick up a pass at the Independence Visitor Center at 6th and Market, or check it out online at www.independence-visitorcenter.com.

### Clothespin Statue
### You Can't Miss It!

Philadelphia had artist Claes Oldenburg make this jumbo clothespin to celebrate the city's 200th birthday in 1976. It stands an eye-popping 45 feet tall and weighs ten tons. If you use your imagination, the jumbo clothespin looks like two people embracing, to honor the "City of Brotherly Love." And the two sides of the big silver fastener on top stand for the numbers "76." Whether you love it or hate it, you can't walk by City Hall without staring at it!

### Columbus Statue
### Columbus Never Looked Like This!

There are lots of statues honoring Christopher Columbus, but this one really stands out—and *up*! It's a three-sided, steel obelisk rising 106 feet in the air, topped by a flag that combines the colors of Spain and Italy. It was built in 1992 to celebrate the 500th anniversary of the explorer's journey to America. At night, lights glow in and through the open spaces of the panels. Find it in the International Sculpture Garden at Penn's Landing.

## Comcast Center
## Wacky Wall!

Who are these people riding on a giant pencil?! They're part of the entertainment on Comcast Center's 83 foot by 25 foot lobby videowall. The *Comcast Experience* is made up of thousands of hours of ever-changing, realistic imagery and is displayed 18 hours a day. This is an attraction not to be missed!

## Congress Hall
### A Capital Decade

Once the Philadelphia County Courthouse, Congress Hall was where Congress met from 1790-1800. The city served as the nation's capital during those ten important years. It's where George Washington and John Adams were inaugurated as president, and the Bill of Rights was added to the Constitution. You can view the authentically-restored chambers of the Senate and House of Representatives and pretend that you were there during this exciting time.

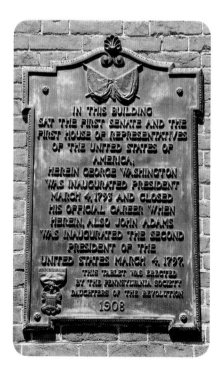

## Constitution
### Supreme Law of the Unites States

The U.S. Constitution is a set of rules that was written in 1787 and replaced the Articles of Confederation. Leaders in the young nation met to define the basic rights of the people and how the government should be run. Fifty-five delegates attended, but only 39 "Framers," or signers, signed the Constitution into law on September 17, 1787. Among them were Ben Franklin, George Washington, and James Madison, Jr.

## Dad Vail Regatta
### Row, Row, Row Your Boat

What is this strange-sounding event? The Dad Vail Regatta is the largest college rowing event in the entire country. More than 100 colleges and up to 500 sculls (light boats) take part every year in May on the city's Schuylkill River. It all started in 1934 when two men with ties to the University of Pennsylvania decided to hold a race and award a trophy. Harry Emerson Vail, nicknamed "Dad," was a coach and close friend to one of the men. The regatta race was proudly named in his honor.

## Declaration House
### Writer Whiz

In the summer of 1776, Thomas Jefferson rented two rooms in this house for the task of writing the first draft of the Declaration of Independence. The original house was torn down and this replica was built in 1975. You can watch a film on the drafting of the Declaration of Independence and see Jefferson's second floor bedroom and parlor with a reproduction of his desk and chair. The house is on 7th and Market Streets and it's free!

## Declaration of Independence
### Happy Birthday, America!

This important document, written in the summer of 1776, was really a letter to the King of England. The American colonists were tired of England telling them what to do and ordering them to pay taxes. The Declaration of Independence stated that America wanted to split off from England and delegates from all the colonies signed it. On July 4, 1776, Congress made it official, and our nation was born on that date. Happy Birthday, America!

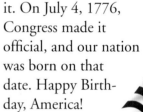

### Delaware River
### A Famous Christmas Crossing

The Delaware River is the longest un-dammed river east of the Mississippi and runs along the length of Philadelphia. It carried Philly superstars William Penn and later Ben Franklin to the Market Street Wharf, now known as Penn's Landing. But it made big-time history on December 25, 1776. That's when George Washington and 2,400 soldiers crossed the Delaware at a spot 25 miles from Philadelphia to success-fully fight the British in the Revolutionary War. You can take tours and watch a movie at Washington Crossing Historic Park.

### Dizzy
### Who's Zooming Who?

Looking up, are you spinning and grin-ning? Or is it more a stomach-churning, head-turning feeling? You may need to sit down and relax after this glimpse of down-town Philadelphia!

### Dolley Todd Madison
### She Slept Here!

Dolley Todd Madison was the wife of James Madison, the 4th President of the United States and is famous for having a portrait of George Washington removed from the White House before the British torched it during the War of 1812. But before she married Madison, Dolley lived in Philadelphia with her first husband, John Todd before he died of yellow fever in 1793. You can visit the Todd House on the corner of 4th and Walnut Streets and see for yourself how the middle class lived in the 18th century. Tickets are available at the Independence Visitor Center.

## Downtown Buildings
## Offices Galore!

Look at how packed these buildings are in Center City, Philly's downtown area. Philadelphia is the sixth most populated city in the U.S. and the largest city in the state; so many businesses want to have their headquarters and offices in this important financial center. And with only 135.6 square miles of land to go around, that's a whole lotta buildings jammed into downtown!

## Drexel Dragon
## Danger!

Don't get too close to this fire-breathing dragon or you just might get burned! A well-known sculptor named Eric Berg created this 14-foot-long, two-ton dragon for Drexel University in 2002. The Drexel mascot is called *Mario the Magnificent*, named for Mario V. Mascioli, who attended every single Drexel men's basketball game for 20 years before he died in 2005. Now that's one loyal fan. Look for other Eric Berg sculptures around Philadelphia, such as *Massa* the gorilla, and *Warthog* at the Philadelphia Zoo.

## Eagles, Flying High
### The Philadelphia Eagles
### Football Team

The American bald eagle is the symbol for our country, and it's also the name for Philadelphia's football team. The club started in 1933 and plays at Lincoln Financial Field. Their colors are midnight green, black, silver, and white. The mascot is a giant eagle called *Swoop*.

## Eakins, Thomas
### Really Famous Painter

Born in Philadelphia in 1844, Thomas Eakins loved two things: art and rowing. He almost became a professional oarsman, or rower, but instead devoted his life to painting. He's famous today for his realistic series of paintings and sketches of men rowing on the Schuylkill River. Also, the annual Thomas Eakins Head of the Schuylkill Regatta was started in 1971 to honor his artwork and love for the sport.

## Eastern State Penitentiary
### Bone-chilling Prison

Doesn't this gloomy room look like it's in a dungeon? Actually, it was the prison cell at Eastern State Penitentiary of Al Capone, one of America's most famous gangsters! Eastern State Penitentiary was built in 1829, and was the first prison to place men in their own cells. It's now a museum, so you can visit and enjoy the interactive exhibits where you get to play guard on the top tower catwalk or eavesdrop on the sounds of actual prison life.

## Edgar Allan Poe's House
## One Scary Writer

The author of spooky stories like *The Black Cat* and *The Pit and the Pendulum* lived in Philadelphia for only one year, but made a lasting impression. Poe is known as the father of the modern detective story, and many of his tales have been turned into classic horror movies. You can tour his three-story brick house at the Edgar Allan Poe National Historic Site, or go next door where you can view a film about his life. Check out the statue of the raven (the name of his famous poem). It will give you a chill!

## Elfreth's Alley
## One of Our Nation's Oldest Streets

Explore 300 years of history by taking a walk down one of our nation's oldest residential streets, Elfreth's Alley. Thirty-two homes, which make up the narrow alleyway, were built between 1728 -1836 and you can visit two of them! Houses 124 and 126 are part of the Elfreth's Alley Museum where you can hear stories about what life was like for the working-class in colonial Philadelphia. This is a charming walk that shouldn't be missed!

## Fairmount Park Welcome Center

You can't hope to see and do everything in Fairmount Park in one day. With over 8,500 acres, 63 separate parks, a large collection of art, and two million trees (yup, someone really counted them all), it's simply too large. But the Fairmount Park Welcome Center will give you the information you need about all the fun things that are available. Located at Love Park, come on in and pick up brochures, purchase tickets, check out the artwork, and watch a video. The information counter also answers questions about attractions across the entire Delaware Valley, so this is a perfect place to plan your day!

## Fireman's Hall Museum
### Really Hot Stuff

How would you like to tour a real 1876 firehouse and get to slide down the brass fire pole? At Fireman's Hall Museum you can. You can learn all about the history of Philadelphia's fire fighting by taking a tour. There are some sizzling hot exhibits that showcase fire engines, parade hats, fire hose nozzles, and an old wooden pumper. In the *KidZone* you can play firefighter, and buy coloring books, puzzles, stickers, books, and even a Firefighter Faith doll.

## Fort Mifflin
## Cannons, and Barracks, and Ghosts, oh my!

Only one battle was fought at Fort Mifflin in 1777 but it lasted 5 weeks, and more than 10,000 cannon balls were fired at it by the British! This long battle was important because during that time British supply ships were delayed and General George Washington was able to retreat to Valley Forge. Be sure to visit the casemates or "dungeons," the 1812 room in the Officer's Quarters, and the museum in the Soldie]rs' Barracks. But be careful. You might bump into a ghost! Fort Mifflin is called one of the most haunted places in the country!

## First Bank in the United States
## Money Mansion!

What if every state in the U.S. used different coins and bills? That was the exact problem with each of the original thirteen colonies. Alexander Hamilton, Secretary of the Treasury, proposed creating a national bank and the First Bank of the United States was built in 1797. The grand-looking structure was the oldest bank building in America, and later became the home of the Civil War Museum.

## Franklin Court
### Go Underground

There's a lot to see and do at this museum honoring the life and accomplishments of Ben Franklin. Unfortunately, nothing remains of the Founding Father's first home in Philadelphia, but architect Robert Venturi created a steel skeleton outline of the building called "Ghost House." In two adjoining houses that Franklin rented, you can find a Colonial-period print shop and postal museum. And don't forget the underground museum where you can listen to famous historical figures talk about Ben Franklin and watch a film "starring" the great man himself. Well, an actor who looks just like him!

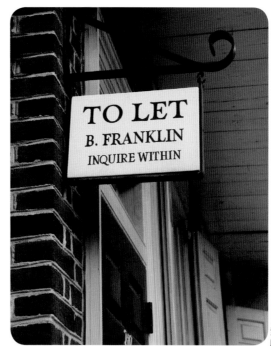

## Franklin Institute & Science Museum
### A Hair-Raising Place!

You and your parents will love this science museum founded in honor of Ben Franklin. Better get here early so you can enjoy as many of the interactive exhibits and attractions as possible. Walk through the world's largest artificial heart (large enough to fit a 220-foot-tall giant!), or watch your hair go crazy in the static electricity exhibit. Sit in the cockpit of a T-33 jet trainer, or ride to nowhere on a 350-ton Baldwin steam locomotive. And before you go, check out Ben Franklin's famous lightning rod and 30-foot-tall statue in the main rotunda.

## Franklin Square Park Carousel
### Take a Twirl

This park is a perfect place to take a break from visiting so many historical buildings. You can play 18 holes of miniature golf, or try the amazing Cake Shake, a milkshake made with Butterscotch Krimpet Tastycakes. Be sure to take a ride on the Philadelphia Park *Liberty Carousel*, with over 30 animals to choose from!

## Free Library of Philadelphia Children's Department, So Many Books!

The city of Philadelphia had no free public library up until the late nineteenth century. Dr. William Pepper (sorry, not the soda guy!) persuaded his rich uncle to give the city

$225,000 to build one. In 1894 the main library opened, and today the Children's Department is famous for the largest collection of children's books, over 65,000! It also carries books for kids in 52 languages. Free tours are given every weekday at 11 a.m. "Check it out."

## George Washington
## He Watches Over Philly

George Washington is known as the "Father of His Country" for the important roles he played in America's early history. Born in Virginia in 1732, he became the first President of the United States in 1789. Shortly after his inauguration, the Capital was moved to Philadelphia and he served two terms here. He was the only President not to have lived in the White House because it was built after his death in 1799. See if you can find this statue on the Ben Franklin Parkway.

### Germantown White House
### One Fighting Place

This elegant, 3-story mansion in the Germantown section of Philadelphia has a fascinating and "fighting" history. When the British occupied the city during the Revolutionary War, a British general named Sir William Howe made the house his headquarters. The Battle of Germantown took place right outside, with muskets firing from upstairs windows! George Washington lived in this house in 1793 and 1794, making it the oldest presidential residence in our country. Come see interactive exhibits when you take a free tour at 5442 Germantown Avenue.

### Grave of Ben Franklin
### Penny Toss

Where is Ben Franklin's tombstone? The city's most famous and best-loved Founding Father is buried at Christ Church Burial Ground. Franklin attended Christ Church and even organized the lottery to raise money for the remarkable 200-foot steeple. Ben Franklin was famous for his quote, "A penny saved is a penny earned," so be sure to honor him by tossing a penny or two on his grave for luck. Christ Church earns an amazing $500 or so in change a year from this tradition!

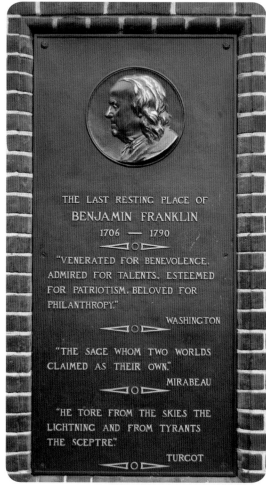

THE LAST RESTING PLACE OF
BENJAMIN FRANKLIN
1706 — 1790

"VENERATED FOR BENEVOLENCE. ADMIRED FOR TALENTS. ESTEEMED FOR PATRIOTISM. BELOVED FOR PHILANTHROPY."
WASHINGTON

"THE SAGE WHOM TWO WORLDS CLAIMED AS THEIR OWN."
MIRABEAU

"HE TORE FROM THE SKIES THE LIGHTNING AND FROM TYRANTS THE SCEPTRE."
TURGOT

## Guess Who?
## Mystery History Person

Are you up for playing detective? If so, then scope out this 15,000-pound sculpture and try to guess who it is. Look at the eye glasses, lightning bolts, and kites on the nearby columns. Do those clues give you an idea who this famous person was? The sculpture is located at 16th and Arch Streets, and you can turn to page 45 for the answer if you're stumped!

### His Honor the Mayor Frank Rizzo (1920-1991)
### Monster Mural of Mayor Rizzo

Frank Rizzo was one of the city's most colorful and famous mayors. He was the 93rd Mayor of Philadelphia and served in the 1970s for two terms. This huge mural of Frank Rizzo was painted in 1995 by Diane Keller and is a popular spot for meetings and speeches. It's on 9th and Montrose in the middle of Italian Market, His Honor's old neighborhood.

### Hoagies
### Hogs & Hokey-Pokey?

A hoagie's known by lots of names, like submarine, hero, grinder, or torpedo. It began in Philadelphia as the hoagie, and it's a super-big cold cuts and cheese sandwich served on a long bun. People believe that the name may have come from "Hoggie," a sandwich eaten by the shipyard workers on Hog Island. Or it could have started with the street vendors called hokey-pokey men. Whatever name it goes by, the hoagie is a mouth-watering treat that's enjoyed in Philly and all across the country!

### Horse-and-Carriage Ride
### '76 Carriage Company

For a fun way to go back in time, why not take a horse-and-carriage ride? The shiny black and red carriages line up on Chestnut and 6th Streets across from Independence Hall, and a tour winds its bouncy way through the narrow streets of the Historic Area. They even give you a blanket to use in the winter!

## Hospital, Pennsylvania
### Where Can You Find Ben Franklin?

Ben Franklin worked hard to raise money to build the first hospital in the nation to care for the "sick-poor and insane of Philadelphia," which began admitting patients in 1756. He wrote an inscription on the original East Wing cornerstone which can still be read today. If you take the guided tour, take note of the big skylight in the country's first surgical operating room. Doctors could only operate in the bright sun between the hours of 11 and 2, and didn't use anesthesia until the 1840s. (*Ouch!*) See if you can spot the two busts of Franklin in the old building.

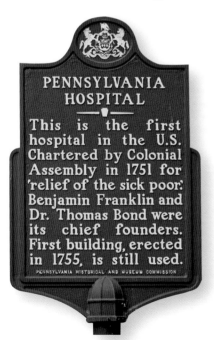

## Hot Air Balloon
### Up, Up and Away!

The first hydrogen balloon flight in North America took place on January 9, 1793. Famous French "aeronaut" Jean Pierre Blanchard lifted off from the old Walnut Street Jail in Philadelphia, as President Washington, John Adams, Thomas Jefferson, James Madison, and the entire city watched in awe and celebrated. He took just one passenger with him, a little black dog! Blanchard flew for 46 minutes until he touched down in Woodbury, New Jersey, fifteen miles away. It was an aviation historic first.

## Independence Hall
### Baby America, Born Here

This red brick building with clock tower and steeple is one of America's most historic places. It started out in 1756 as the Pennsylvania State House, but was renamed after awesome things happened here. George Washington was appointed the head of the new Continental Army inside the hall's Assembly Room. It's also where 56 courageous men signed the Declaration of Independence. Check out the only two remaining original pieces of furniture, George Washington's "Rising Sun" chair, and Ben Franklin's desk.

## Independence Living History Center
### Bring Your Curiosity!

Come see real archeologists work on pieces discovered at Philadelphia excavation sites at the Independence Living History Center Laboratory. There are more than one million artifacts of the city's buried treasures and you can watch the archeologists clean, mend, and label animal bones and ceramic fragments, and ask them questions, too! Be sure to watch the movie, *1776*, for more background on historic Philly.

## Independence Visitor Center
## All Questions Welcome!

This is a perfect place to start your sight-seeing tours of the city. The center is located right outside Independence National Historic Park and offers free tickets to Independence Hall. Ask questions about where to go at the front desk, grab a bite to eat at the indoor or outdoor cafés, or buy fun stuff at the gift shop. Don't miss the 30-minute movie, *Independence*, showing in the center's three theaters. It makes the city's Founding Fathers come alive.

## Independence Park
## Seriously Impressive History!

Independence National Historical Park is over 55 acres on 20 city blocks, and includes Independence Hall, Liberty Bell Center, Independence Visitors Center, Franklin Court, the First and Second Banks of the United States, and so many other famous historic sites. Kids visiting the Park can become a Junior Ranger by completing fun activities, or can turn into an archeologist themselves and dig for artifacts, or learn how to play the glass armonica, a cool musical instrument invented by Benjamin Franklin.

## Independence Seaport Museum
## Ahoy, Matey!

Turn into a world-class sailor at Philly's maritime museum. You'll get to view lots of ship models, figureheads, and other neat nautical stuff, and crawl through a 22-foot 19th- century light sailing ship. Tour the mighty cruiser USS *Olympia*, or the 318-foot-long "guppy class" sub, the USS *Becuna*. You don't want to miss the NEWTSUIT, a submarine you can actually wear! If that doesn't float your boat, climb into an immigrant's cold, hard bunk to find out how it felt to travel in the steerage section of a ship. Or hop in a scull and row along the Schuylkill River.

## Japanese House and Garden
## What, No Walls?

Shofuso is the only 17th-century house of its kind outside of Japan. It was a gift from Japan to America in 1953, and you can see the way a scholar lived 500 years ago by visiting the house and garden at Fairmount Park. There are sliding screens with murals and paper doors, instead of walls and glass. Be sure to take the guided tour so you'll know just what you are looking at!

## Joan of Arc Statue
## Joanie on a Pony!

Doesn't this figure of Joan of Arc look like she's about to gallop into battle? The Fairmount Park Art Association gave this statue to Philadelphia in 1890. Did you know that Joan of Arc is the youngest person to have commanded an army? She was only 17 years old when she led the French army during the Hundred Years' War in the 1400's. You can find her statue in Fairmount Park.

## Italian Market
## Oldest Outdoor Market

Begun in the late 1800s by Italians settling in Philadelphia, this area of about 10 city blocks offers everything from cheeses, fresh pastas, and pastries, to meats, spices, and fruits. It's noisy and colorful, with vendors crowding the sidewalks, selling live crabs, caged chickens, and fish. Come for the annual 9th Street Italian Market Festival in May and enjoy the biggest block party ever, with the annual procession of saints, live music and entertainment, face painting, and other kid-pleasing activities.

31

## Johnson House Historical Site
## Underground Railroad Stop

The Underground Railroad wasn't really underground! This was a term that was used because escaping slaves and the people who helped them had to hide their actions. The Johnson family were some of the people who offered runaway slaves temporary shelter, food, clothing, and transportation as they fled to freedom. Today, kids can see the recently-discovered hiding places in the attic and on the roof. The Johnson House is on Germantown Avenue.

## Keane, Bil
## Philly "Funnies" Man

Have you ever read (and laughed at) *Family Circus* in the paper? The cartoonist who draws this popular, long-running strip is Bil Keane, who was born in Philadelphia in 1922. He says: "I grew up in that city with a penn by my side—William Penn!" *Family Circus* began in 1960, and now appears in over 1,500 newspapers.

## Keystone State
## Pennsylvania's Nickname

No one knows for sure how Pennsylvania got its nickname but many believe it is because in 1776 delegates from Pennsylvania cast the deciding voted for independence. Without that vote our nation may not have pursued independence from Britain. A keystone is a wedge that holds an arch in place and  Philadelphia held our new nation together.

## Kimmel Center
## Glowing Night-Time Slinky

Well, half of one. That's what the lighted 150-foot glass vaulted rooftop looks like on the Kimmel Center for the Performing Arts. This is the city's main performance space for the Chamber Orchestra, Philly Pops, Opera Company, and the Pennsylvania Ballet. Besides all this great entertainment, you can take a tour and go backstage. How cool is that?

## King of Steaks
## He Invented the Cheesesteak!

"Wit' or wit'-out," onions that is. That's how to order a cheesesteak sandwich at Pat's King of Steaks. Pat Olivieri is the true "King of Steaks" in Philadelphia because he and his brother Henry invented the cheesesteak. They were selling hot dogs at a stand in the Italian Market when they decided to try grilling thinly sliced steak with onions and putting it on an Italian roll. Customers ate it up. Later cheese was added and the first cheesesteak was born! Be sure to try your sandwich "Whiz wit" which is with Cheese Whiz. Try one from his famous restaurant, Pat's King of Steaks, located at 1237 E. Passyunk Avenue.

## Korean War Memorial
## Veteran Tribute

This memorial honors the 610 soldiers from five Pennsylvania Counties who gave their lives in combat during the Korean War. Four 16-foot- tall interior columns list their names, and the four surrounding outer stones are etched with words, pictures, and medals from the war. Also at this site is the statue, *The Final Farewell*, as well as flags and markers. This memorial is located across from the Vietnam Memorial.

### Liberty Bell
### It's Everything it's Cracked Up to Be

What's only three feet tall, weighs 2,080 pounds, and symbolizes freedom in the United States? It's the Liberty Bell. The bell you see today at Liberty Bell Center is actually the third bell that was made for the State House. The first bell cracked during a test ringing; the second had an unsatisfactory pitch; the third bell was finally judged acceptable. No one is sure why, but, sadly, this bell eventually cracked too, and it rang for the last time in 1846 for its annual ringing on George Washington's Birthday.

Did you know that the bell was originally called the State House Bell? It wasn't called the Liberty Bell until the 1830s when a group of people wanted liberty and freedom for slaves. Their inspiration came from the inscription on the bell that reads, "Proclaim Liberty throughout the land unto all the inhabitants thereof."

### Liberty Place
### The Curse of Billy Penn

For years the tallest spot in the Philadelphia skyline had been the statue of William Penn atop City Hall. It was an unwritten rule of respect not to build anything higher than Penn. However, the 945-foot-high skyscraper One Liberty Place broke this rule in 1987, and the "Curse of Billy Penn" started! No Philadelphia professional sports team won a championship for years. Luckily, the 975-foot Comcast Center went up in 2008 with a tiny statue of William Penn on the roof, making the city founder the highest point again. That same year the Phillies won the World Series. The curse was broken!

### Light Show on Broad Street

Broad Street is one of the busiest streets in Philadelphia, and Avenue of the Arts is a section that includes many theaters, concert halls, and performing arts centers. Philadelphia illuminates this section of the city every night with a programmed light show. Be prepared to be dazzled!

### Logan Circle & Swann Fountain Making a Big Splash!

This was one of William Penn's five squares of land to be set aside for parks. It was named for his secretary, James Logan. The centerpiece of Logan Circle is *Swann Memorial Fountain.* There are Native Americans, swans, a fish, turtles, frogs, and water spraying 25 feet into the air! It's a perfect place to wet your toes on a hot summer day. Each of the Native American figures in this fountain represent Philadelphia's three local streams, the Delaware, the Schuylkill, and the Wissahickon.

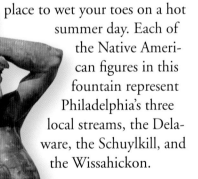

### Lights of Liberty Wowie Zowie!

Want a mega-magical way to experience the history of Philadelphia? Zoom on over to the Historic Philadelphia Center and enjoy the 360-degree, 3-D spectacular attraction called Liberty 360 inside the new PECO Theater. For an even bigger thrill, attend the New Lights of Liberty Show, the first outdoor, nighttime 3-D show ever created. High-tech images of our nation's fight for independence are projected in glorious color on the city's historic buildings. The show runs April through October.

## Masonic Temple
## Top Secret

Doesn't this amazing building remind you of a castle in Transylvania? It's the Masonic Temple, home to one of the oldest—and most secret—organizations in the world. The Free and Accepted Masons were popular during Colonial times in Philadelphia, and many of their members were instrumental in the Revolutionary War. Both George Washington and Ben Franklin were Masons. If you visit the Temple, you can't miss the lavishly decorated Egypt room. The hieroglyphics are so real you'll swear you're actually in ancient Egypt!

## LOVE Sculpture
## Really a Greeting Card?

That's a fact. This 12- x 12-foot sculpture was first designed as a Christmas card in 1964. The LOVE image became so famous that its designer, Robert Indiana, turned it into a ten-ton steel sculpture. It was placed in JFK Plaza, and nicknamed "LOVE Park," to honor the city's 200th birthday in 1976. Since then, the *LOVE* sculpture has earned a special honor in Philly. Can you guess what it is? Find the Answer on page 45.

## Mummers Museum and Mural
## "Welcome to Mummerland!"

Before visiting the Mummers Museum, read all about the Mummers Parade on page 40. And, if you are lucky enough to get a chance to see the parade on New Years day, then you'll know that Mummers are dancing, acting, playful masqueraders who revel in entertaining you! You can see their outlandish award –winning costumes, doll exhibits, and memorabilia at the Mummers Museum on 1100 South 2nd Street.

## Military Museum at New Hall
## War and More

This two-story reconstructed building of 1791 once served as headquarters for the War Department. Come inside and be wowed by displays of Revolutionary War uniforms, weapons, and dioramas of famous battles. The *Marines in the Revolution* exhibit describes the amazing role of the "Leathernecks" from 1775-1781, called that because of their leather collars. Play the "Sea Battle" game on the second floor or view the model of the USS *Constitution*. It's on Chestnut Street and free!

## Mother Bethel Church
## A.M.E. (African Methodist Episcopal)

Back in 1791, former slave Richard Allen purchased a parcel of land on 6th and Lombard Streets and hauled an old blacksmith shop onto it. He then hired carpenters to convert the shop into a church and in 1794, America's first Black Methodist Society held its first service. More than two centuries and four buildings later the Bethel Church continues to serve Philadelphia's African Americans and others. While visiting be sure to view the stained glass windows and the museum's mural.

## Mural Mile
## Celebrate Philly Kids!

Can you believe this amazing mural covers the entire side of an 8-story building? Artist Meg Saligman painted *Tribute to Philadelphia's Youth: Common Thread* in 1997. It was part of the city's Mural Arts Program that was started in 1984 to fight graffiti and beautify its neighborhoods. Since then, more than 3000 murals have been created. No wonder Philadelphia has earned world-wide praise as the "City of Murals." Explore 17 of the most iconic murals along a 2-mile guided walking route from Independence Visitor Center.

## Murray, Jim
## Ronald McDonald House

The very first Ronald McDonald House was created right here by Philadelphian and co-founder Jim Murray in 1974. No, this isn't a place to enjoy a nice juicy hamburger and French fries. It's a place where moms and dads can stay when their kids are being treated at nearby hospitals, and it doesn't cost very much, either. Today, there are more than 200 houses worldwide.

## Mütter Museum
## Not for the Squeamish

Warning: this weird and medically monstrous collection will gross you out! The Mütter Museum at the College of Physicians of Philadelphia contains seriously strange objects. The first thing you'll see is a collection of 139 skulls! Yuk! There's a body of a woman that turned into soap, a cast of joined twins Chang and Eng, and an unbelievable assortment of items swallowed and removed from people's stomachs!

## National Constitution Center
## You be President

Just show up at this center and be sworn in at an interactive inauguration ceremony that's broadcast right behind you! Or maybe you'd rather sit at the Supreme Court bench and decide a case, or walk among the bronze, life-size statues of the men who signed the Constitution. This museum makes learning about the U.S. Constitution way more fun than reading about it in books. Don't leave without seeing the dramatic show, Freedom Rising, which takes you from the American Revolution through the signing of the Constitution.

## National Liberty Museum
### Embrace Different Views

This small, but powerful museum focuses on our country's heritage of freedom and diversity. The 20-foot-tall red glass art, *Flame of Liberty*, by Dale Chihuly, is just one piece of glass art on display that represents how fragile freedom is. *The Jelly Bean People* by Sandy Skoglund reminds us that our differences are only skin deep. There's a new interactive exhibit called *Heroes of Character* that challenges you to make your own heroic decisions. With 78 exhibits, there is lots to see and do.

## National Wildlife Refuge
### The Great Outdoors!

Where can you go every day of the year to explore the resting and feeding areas for a wide variety of birds, animals, wildflowers, plants, and hiking trails galore? The John Heinz National Wildlife Refuge, of course! Kids can learn all about nature through videos, bird watching tours, and field trips. It's all free so break out your hiking boots!

## National Kid's Day Talent Show
### "America Loves Talent"

Kids will be wowed at Philadelphia's National Kid's Day Talent Show, held at Dutch Wonderland in nearby Lancaster. They'll get to watch kids their own age perform magic tricks and gymnastics, sing, dance, and so much more. And Dutch Wonderland is a park that's full of fun roller coasters, terrific water rides, and other exciting attractions. So it's double the entertainment.

## Neon
### It's a Gas, Gas, Gas!

Check out the brilliant glow of these neon signs at the Reading Terminal Market. There are loads more inside. Neon in Greek means "new gas," and the first neon lamps showed up in Paris in 1910. While you're visiting this super-sized market, walk around the 80 different shops and food stalls. Before you go, feed pennies to *Philbert*, the bronze pig in the market center. Everything he collects goes to charity.

## New Year's Day Mummers Parade
### Longest Parade in the U.S.

Philly loves the wacky and wonderful Mummers, and this mural honors 100 years of their annual New Year's Day Parade down Broad Street. The first official parade was on January 1, 1901, and most last as long as 11 hours! There are different groups of Mummers who march. The "Comics" are clowns who start the parade and poke fun at current events. "Fancies" with small floats strut in elaborate costumes. "String bands" play music using banjos, accordions, drums, and other instruments. And the largest groups are the "Fancy brigades" who perform theatrical acts with their finale taking place indoors at the Convention Center. It's jaw dropping!

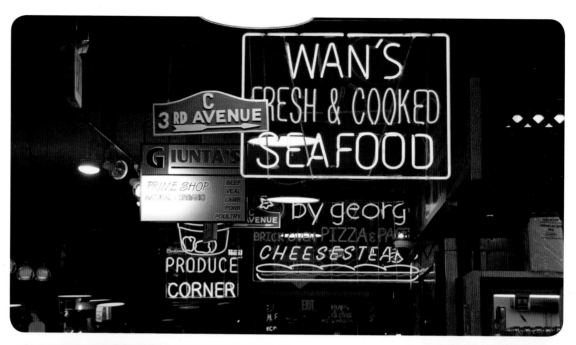

## Oatmeal
## An Urban Legend

The image of the man on the Quaker Oatmeal box has often been said to be William Penn (see a picture of him on page 59). Painted by Haddon Sundblom around 1941, it is really a representation of "a man dressed in Quaker garb." The man is wearing the same kind of clothes that William Penn would have worn. Who knew?

### Once Upon a Nation
### It's Story Time!

Philadelphia history comes alive at 13 free story-telling benches around Independence Mall from May to September. Storytellers ring a special town crier bell at each bench and entertain and educate you with exciting, little-known tales about Betsy Ross, Independence Hall, and African-American abolitionist movement leader James Forte, among others. Be sure to collect your Story Flag from the storyteller. Once you have all 13, go to the Historic Philadelphia Center to collect a prize. This surely beats learning in the classroom!

### Penn's Landing
### It all Started Here

This riverfront park is the spot where both William Penn and Ben Franklin first set foot in Philadelphia. The 37-acre Delaware River waterfront is a perfect place to see tons of pleasure boats and cargo ships, and enjoy views of the 1,750-foot-long Benjamin Franklin Bridge. If you look down the river, you can spot the 1892 USS *Olympia*, the oldest steel warship afloat. Next to it is the submarine USS *Becuna*. Both are currently museum ships. For fun, grab lunch at the four-masted ship, the *Moshulu*, now a restaurant. There's a lot to see and do at one of the world's largest free water ports!

## Pennsylvania Railroad's WW II Statue
## Star of the Station

This imposing bronze sculpture by Walker Hancock stands in the lobby of the 30th Street Train Station. *Pennsylvania Railroad World War II Memorial,* or *Angel of Resurrection,* shows the archangel Michael holding up a fallen soldier in honor of his bravery. The pedestal lists the names of the 1,307 Penn Railroad employees who died in World War II. Hancock created hundreds of works, but this was said to be his favorite.

## Philadelphia 76ers
## Team of Champions

Wilt Chamberlain, Julius Erving, Moses Malone, Maurice Cheeks, and Charles Barkley are arguably the most famous 76ers basketball players. The team plays home games at the Wells Fargo Center from November to April. Their colors are red, royal blue, and white. Hip-Hop is their mascot, the coolest hare (rabbit) around.

## Philadelphia Centennial Exposition
## Step Inside Liberty's Torch!

The very first World's Fair in the U.S. celebrated the 100th anniversary of the signing of the Declaration of Independence. In honor of this important date in American history, France sculpted the Statue of Liberty for the fair. However, it wasn't done in time, so only the colossal arm holding the torch could be displayed. People paid 50 cents to climb a ladder almost 40 feet to reach Liberty's torch. More than ten million visitors from around the world attended the fair. Go to page 44 to find out where you can find a toy replica of Liberty's Arm and Torch.

## Philadelphia Doll Museum
## Toy Joy!

It's all about dolls here, and so much more. The Philadelphia Doll Museum on North Broad Street has over 300 black dolls in its collection. The figures help tell the story of black culture and history throughout the world. You'll find African wooden dolls, black bisque dolls from Germany, and even celebrity dolls like Louise Armstrong and Bill Cosby. You can even take a workshop on Paper Doll Making and Clothes Pin Dolls.

## Philadelphia Flyers
## Broad Street Bullies

Philadelphia's pro hockey team began in 1967, but folded after just one year. They didn't make a comeback until 40 years later when they were known as the Flyers. They're nicknamed the "Broad Street Bullies" because they play home games at the Wells Fargo Center off Broad Street. They've won more games than any other hockey team except for the Montreal Canadiens, and their colors are orange, black and white.

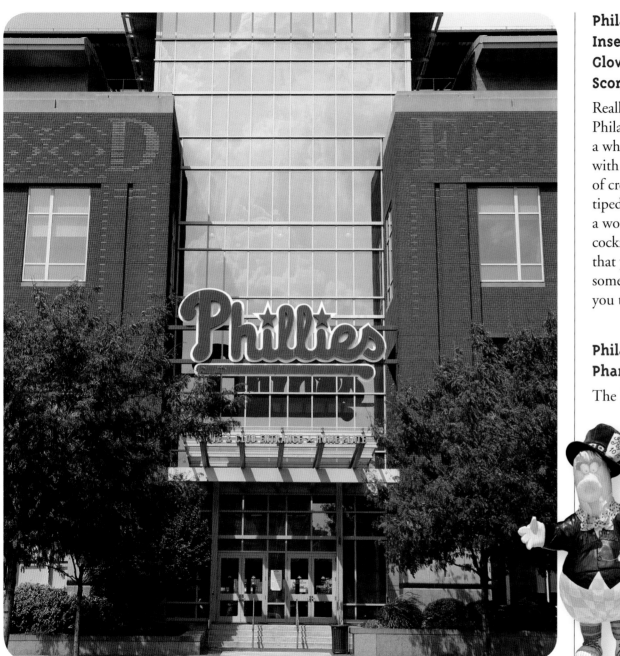

### Philadelphia Insectarium Glow-in-the-Dark Scorpions!

Really? You bet, and Philadelphia's only all-bug museum has a whole lot more. This place is swarming with more than 50 live species, thousands of creepy crawlies like tarantulas, giant centipedes, even assassin bugs. Killer! There's a working beehive, a kitchen teeming with cockroaches, and a man-made spider web that you can play in. You can even hold some of the bugs! That will certainly give you the "heebie-jeebies!"

### Philadelphia Phillies Phanatic-al Fans

The Philadelphia Phillies were first called the Quakers in 1883, but became the Philadelphians, or Phillies, a year later. They play at Citizens Bank Park and their colors are red, white, and blue. Their mascot, Phanatic, is a world-famous fat, furry character who keeps all the fans cheering.

## Quakers
## Friends Indeed!

The Quakers, also known as Friends, believe in a peaceful way of life and a simple way to worship. The Arch Street Meeting House is the oldest and largest Quaker meeting house in the world. It was built in 1804 on land that William Penn gave them in 1693 and is still being used today. Back then, young Quaker boys and girls had to use separate stairs to reach the balcony, and a 4-inch-high "modesty board" ran along the girls' staircase to keep their ankles from accidentally showing! Be sure to view the slide show about William Penn and video on Quakerism.

## Please Touch Museum
## Hands on, for Sure!

Discover six gigantic discovery zones. You can explore a television studio, a hospital, a supermarket, or slide down the rabbit hole to have tea with Alice in Wonderland! Take a ride on the colorful Dentzel Carousel, and look carefully at the 40-foot-tall Statue of Liberty's arm and torch in the Great Hall. It's made entirely with toys, games, and junk! Can you spot the baseball bat and the Santa Claus figure? What else do you see? The museum is located in Fairmount Park.

## Poor Richard's Almanack

Benjamin Franklin printed the first copy of his yearly *Poor Richard's Almanack* in 1732, and it became an instant bestseller. Colonial Americans loved to read the weather forecasts, household hints, puzzles, poems, and sayings. One of Franklin's most famous quotes was, "Early to bed, early to rise, makes a man healthy, wealthy, and wise." *Poor Richard's Almanack* lasted until 1758 and sold an average of 10,000 copies a year. Who was Richard? He wasn't real. Franklin invented him!

## QUESTIONS
## find the answers!

- Where can you find the world's largest artificial heart? Page 24.
- What was the Billy Penn Curse? Page 34.
- What magic happens on the Ben Franklin Bridge when the trains go across? Page 7.
- Where can you find a second swinging, ringing Liberty Bell? Page 11.
- What are the ingredients of a Philly Cheesesteak? Page 10.
- What kind of submarine can you put on and wear? Page 30.
- Who does the Hip Hop Hare root for? Page 43.
- Where can you pet a stingray? Page 4.
- Where can you go to be sworn in as president? Page 38.
- Where is the rowing center of the U.S.? Page 9.
- Where is Ben Franklin buried and what is tossed on his grave? Page 26.
- Who was the only U.S. President not to live in the White House? Page 25.
- Who stands guard outside the Tomb of the Unknown Soldier? Page 54.

## ANSWERS
## find the questions!

Find the mystery questions in this book!

**Page 6**
**Answer:** University of Pennsylvania

**Page 8**
**Answer:** 244, believe it or not!

**Page 11**
**Answer:** Benjamin Franklin, Francis Hopkinson, Joseph Hewes, George Ross, Dr. Benjamin Rush

**Page 18**
**Answer:** She helped save the Gilbert Stuart painting of President George Washington during the War of 1812.

**Page 27**
**Answer:** Benjamin Franklin.

**Page 36**
**Answer:** It's considered the most popular (and copied!) statue in Philly.

**Page 48**
**Answer:** The entire pig's head! (Scrapple)

**Page 50**
**Answer:** They make 130 million of these a year! (Tastykakes section)

## Quick Facts

### You've Gotta be Kidding Me!

Root beer, street vendors selling ices and sandwiches (the "hokey pokey man"), and men and women eating together in cafés for the very first time were introduced at Philadelphia's Centennial Exposition in 1876. And some visitors lined up for their very first taste of an exotic treat that came wrapped in foil and sold for a dime. What was it? The banana!

### Moving the U.S. Capital
### Make up your mind!

Think our U.S. capital has always been in Washington? Wrong! Under the Constitution, the capital was first located in New York City from March 1789 - December 1790. But then Philly became its proud home from 1790 - 1800. The capital finally ended up in Washington, D.C., where it's remained ever since. (Whew!)

### Dubble Bubble Boo-Boo

The very first bubble gum sold in the U.S. was invented by mistake. Walter E. Diemer, a Philadelphia Fleer Chewing Gum Company accountant, was experimenting when he accidentally created bubble gum. Since the food coloring used by the factory was pink, that's what he went with. He wrapped one hundred pieces, sold them for a penny, and the rest is bubblicious history.

## Digging Philly

If you dig straight down from Philadelphia to the other side of the globe, where do you think you'll come up? The middle of the Indian Ocean.

## Go Nuts at Fairmount Park

Two million trees in this park add up to tons and tons of nuts! Who picked them up? School kids came to an annual event called "Nutting Day" every year to collect the thousands of fallen walnuts, hickory nuts, and chestnuts. The very last event happened on October 8, 1870, and 60,000 kids attended!

### Philly Fabulous World Firsts:

Cheesesteak

Children's Hospital

Computer

Flag of the United States

Life Insurance

Lightning Rod

Root Beer

Sunday School

Women's Magazine

## Ride the Ducks
## Quack Attack

For a totally wet and wild tour of Philadelphia's historic sights and Delaware River, hop on a "duck" and go quackers! Ride the Ducks is 70 minutes of nonstop fun on land and water, aboard an amphibious-designed vehicle based on the WWII DUKW. Tours run from mid-March through November. Board at 6th and Market Streets and be prepared to sing, make duck sounds, and scream with laughter.

### Philly Firsts in America:

Balloon Flight

Bank

Volunteer Fire Company

Hospital

Paper Mill

Pharmacy

First Public Grammar School

Sunday School

Theater Company

World's Fair

Zoo

## Rocky Statue
## "Gonna Fly Now"

If you visit the Philadelphia Museum of Art, be sure to get your picture taken with the larger-than-life bronze statue of boxer Rocky Balboa before reliving that famous scene from Rocky. Then run, jog, or if you have to walk up the 72 "Rocky Steps" to the top, turn around and triumphantly raise your arms above your head! Actor Sylvester Stallone commissioned this statue and it appeared in the movies *Rocky III* and *Rocky V*.

## Rodin Museum
## The Thinker

Have you ever seen the statue called *The Thinker*? Famous French sculptor Auguste Rodin made it, and you can see many more of his realistic statues at the Rodin Museum, located on the Benjamin Franklin Parkway. It is said to be among the most famous sculptures in the world! Before entering the museum, take a look at the *Gates of Hell* sculpture, with more than 180 figures, and see if you can find *The Thinker*.

## Rosenbach Museum & Library
## Where the Wild Things Are!

Guess what's hiding inside this 1865 townhouse and adjoining building? Not only tons of Persian rugs, antiques, and paintings, but the best collection of Maurice Sendak books, drawings, and family historical objects! Take part in tours, storytelling sessions, and a special program in March that's all about the book *Where the Wild Things Are*. Kids will love interacting with the dramatic retelling of Max's adventure, and seeing original art that made it into this classic book, as well as other beloved stories.

## Rowhouses
## Sticking Together!

Did you know that the very first rowhouse was built in Philadelphia? They were one-to four-story buildings that were joined together, and they looked exactly alike. Not only were your neighbors connected through walls, but you'd also have a row of outhouses running through the back yards! And, meals were cooked in basement fireplaces. (Talk about smokin'!) Thomas Carstairs developed the very first rowhouses in the early 1800s, and they immediately became one of the most popular forms of housing in Philly.

## Schuylkill River Sculling
## Racing on the Water

The Schuylkill (say it SKOO-kull) is the city's second river and winds past historic Boathouse Row. People use oars called sculls, and scull races involve crews of twos or fours trying to come in first on a marked stretch of the river. Catch races from dawn to dusk from February to October. Exciting!

## Scrapple

Breakfast scrapple originally comes from the Pennsylvania Dutch and looks like a mushy meatloaf that's pan-fried before it's served. Called "everything but the oink," it's made with cornmeal, flour, seasonings, and the heart, liver and scraps of a pig. There's a secret ingredient that makes this an "eat-if you-dare" food! Flip to the Answer on page 45 to find out.

## Sesame Place
### "Be a Kid"

Big Bird, Elmo, Bert, and Ernie invite you to Sesame Place. It honors all the lovable characters from *Sesame Street*. Go on over 17 dry rides, 10 water rides, and scream on the Vapor Trail roller coaster. Take in shows and all the attractions from May through late October. It's Cookie Monster*ific* and perfect for the whole family.

## Signers Walk
### Check Out the John Hancocks!

On Chestnut Street, between 6th and 7th Streets, are plaques on the sidewalk that honor the 56 members of the Continental Congress who signed the Declaration of Independence. Each plaque shows the name, signature, and picture of each man who made history in 1776-1777.

## Skyscrapers & Schooner
### How High and How Large?

Even though there is no height requirement for a building to be called a skyscraper, it does need to stand out in the city's skyline and look like it is scraping the sky. Philly's tallest skyscraper is the Comcast Center. One Liberty Plaza is the city's second-largest building. And talking super-sized, the world's largest four-masted tall ship still afloat is the *Moshulu*. The "restaurant ship" is permanently moored at Penn's Landing, and you can hop onboard for a great meal or tour!

## SMITH
### The Kid's Play Place in the Park

This kid-friendly center in East Fairmount Park has four different playgrounds, a three-story playhouse called *The Mansion*, and the *Giant Wooden Slide*. Children five and under can spend hours in the 24,000-square-foot playhouse, riding trikes in the basement, "cooking" in the kitchen, or "driving" a train. Outside, kids up to ten can fly down the wooden slide, scream at the jumbo spider web, or climb on or swing from over 50 state-of-the-art pieces of play equipment. Smith is in Fairmount Park.

## Swan Boats
### Bird's the Word!

There's nothing more fun than paddling in Victorian-style swan boats, and the city offers two places where you can do just that. You can paddle around Bird Lake at the Philadelphia Zoo, or take a ride at Penn's Landing Marina. The Paddle Penn's Landing Program offers swan boat rides Thursday through Sunday in the afternoons, departing just south of the Independence Seaport Museum.

## Tastykakes
### Wickedly Good

Tastykakes are a true Philly treat. Bite into any one of the Tastykakes, Butterscotch Krimpets, or Chocolate Juniors and you'll be hooked. Started in Philadelphia in 1914 by a Pittsburgh baker and a Boston egg salesman, the small Tasty Baking Company turned out 100 cakes their very first day in business. Today, they bake over 4.8 million cakes, donuts, cookies, and pies each day. Their top-selling item is the Peanut Butter Kandy Kake. How many do they make a year? You'll have to flip to the Answer on page 45 to find out!

## The Signer Statue
### Singing for Happiness

Philly insiders call this "The Singer," rather than *The Signer*, because it looks like he's singing into a microphone! But this 9½-foot bronze statue really symbolizes the pride and courage of *all* the brave men who signed the Declaration of Independence in 1776, as well as the U.S. Constitution in 1787. *The Signer* looks up to the skies as he holds a scroll that represents the two important documents. Visit the Signers Garden at the corner of 5th and Chestnut Streets to see this statue.

### The Starman in the Ancient Garden
### "Beam me down, Scotty!"

What alien object from outer space has crash-landed at Washington Square West? It's an amazing and mysterious bronze face streaming from the heavens by Brower Hatcher. The steel mesh comet tail rises 27 feet in the air and contains objects from Starman's journey, like animals and even a small person! Some people think the sculptor was making a statement about the changes in civilization. What do you think?

### Train Station
### L-o-o-ng Full Name

This 21-story building is called One Penn Center at Suburban Station and was originally built in 1930. It's the main railroad station in Philadelphia and also the underground commuter rail station, along with Amtrak. Known for short as One Penn Center, it has a large concourse level, and lots of retail shops, restaurants, offices, and a nice Art Deco front!

### Trolleys, by Golly
### See the City!

How about hopping on a Victorian-style trolley or a double-decker, open-top Big Bus to see the city? The Philadelphia Trolley Works offers these two unique ways to tour historic spots, and you can board at

any one of the 20 spots along the way. See the Historic Area, Ben Franklin Parkway, Fairmount Park, or the Philadelphia Zoo, and lots more, for one low price. Or take a SEPTA trolley operated by the city and create a tour of your own.

## U.S. Mint
## Millions of Coins

Who doesn't love money, and the Philadelphia Mint is the best place to learn all about it. There are currently four mints in the U.S., but the Philadelphia Mint is the largest, not only in America, but also in the world! The original was built in 1792, and its very first coins were struck from the household silver of President George Washington. The current mint was built in 1969 and has a visitors' gallery with medals from the country's wars, as well as a shop that sells special coins. Come see how the Mint creates all the pennies, nickels, dimes, and quarters that you feed your piggy bank, and best of all, it's *free*.

## Union Jack
## One of America's First Flags

Why is a British flag flying from a Colonial home? Up until 1776 and our independence, colonists were still subjects of King George III. The British Union flag flew over all the New World colonies. Many in Philadelphia displayed this flag as a sign of loyalty to their home country. Many different flags were flown in the colonies, but there was no official national flag until *after* the Revolutionary War when our young nation designed its own.

## United States Post Office
### You've Got Mail!

William Penn may have established the first post office in Pennsylvania, but it was Ben Franklin who figured out how to really make it work. Letters used to take 14 days to travel from New York City to Philadelphia! While Ben was Postmaster General he cut delivery time in half by establishing better routes and having the mail wagon travel day and night. Stamps weren't used then so he came up with a way to charge for letters based on weight and destination. It's fitting that his face is on the very first 5¢ U.S postage stamp in 1847.

## University of Pennsylvania
### A U.S. First

Did you know that Ben Franklin was a founding father of the University of Pennsylvania? It's true! Back in 1749 Ben organized a bunch of leaders of Philadelphia and together they opened the Academy. This institution later became the University of Pennsylvania, the first university in the United States. The mascot for Penn is the Quaker.

## Unknown Soldier
### Revolutionary War Heroes

Jean-Antoine Houdon's famous bronze sculpture of George Washington stands guard outside the Tomb of the Unknown Revolutionary War Soldier in Washington Square. An eternal flame flickers in front of Washington to honor the Father of Our Country, as well as all of the unidentified soldiers of the Revolutionary War. The monument was built in 1957.

## Valley Forge
### Birthplace of the American Army

The first months of the winter of 1777-1778 that George Washington spent in Valley Forge were times of great despair as he watched his soldiers grow weak and weary from frigid weather, lack of food, inadequate clothing, and disease.

Fortunately, under George Washington's leadership, conditions improved and his men began training under Baron Friedrich von Steuben. The soldiers emerged as a strong and confident army. Although no battle was fought here, it is considered the turning point of the Revolutionary War. Visit the Welcome Center at Valley Forge National Historical Park to see a short film, view exhibits, and then take a trolley tour of the grounds. It's only 17 miles from Philly and worth the short trip!

GEORGE W. ABEY
ROWLAND J. ADAMOLI
JOHN E. ADDISON
RAYMOND J. AHERN, JR.
FRANCIS J. ALBERTS
KENNETH E. ALESHIRE
ROBERT S. ALEXANDER
ANTHONY ALLEN
JAMES J. ALLEN
JOHN B. ALLEN
RICHARD C. ALLEN
ROY ALLEN
JOE AMOS
GEORGE J. ANDERSON
JAMES ANDERSON
JOHN R. ANELI
BRUCE F. ANELLO
CHARLES F. ANTONELLY

RONNIE E. ASH
CARLOS ASHLOCK
HOWARD T. ATKINSON, JR.
EDWARD M. ATKUCUNAS
DAVID BAKER
DONALD BAKER
ROBERT L. BANKS
DONALD J. BARNES
WILLIAM C. BAROTT
KAROL R. BAUER
FRED O. BAUGH, JR.
HARRY J. BEADLE, JR.
MICHAEL L. BEASLEY
WILLIAM G. BEHAN, JR.
GEORGE J. BELANCIN
CHARLES A. BELL
WILLIAM BELL
JOHN F. BENSE, JR.
RICHARD L. BARIGLIO

JOEL BERNSTEIN
MICHAEL F. BINGHAM
JACK BITTING
WILLIAM B. BLACKMON, JR.
STEPHEN P. BLANCHETT
CHARLES J. BLANCO
LURAL L. BLEVINS, III
LAWRENCE J. BOLGER
JAMES I. BOWDREN
WILLIS S. BOWMAN, JR.
JAMES R. BOYLE
LAWRENCE A. BRANIGAN
JOHN A. BRAXTON
BRYANT BRAYBOY, JR.
PATRICK J. BRESLIN
ROBERT R. BRETT
WILLIAM M. BRIDGEFO
RONALD D. BRIGGS

PHILLIP L. BROCKMAN
FREDDIE BROOKINS
ZACKRIE BROOKINS, JR.
RICHARD W. BROOKS, III
ALFRED L. BROWN
KENNETH W. BROWN
MARTIN BROWN
WALTER BROWN
WILLIAM J. BROWN
WILLIAM L. BROWN
ROBERT F. BRULTE, JR.
HECTOR W. BRYAN
CHARLES J. BUCKLEY
MARSHALL BURKE, JR.
SAMUEL N. BURTON
MANFRED F. CAMAROTE
ROBERT J. CAMPBELL
RONALD J. CAMPBELL

ROBERT J. CARA
TYREE CARDWELL
PATRICK J. CARNELL
WILLIAM H. CARPENTER, JR.
ROBERT H. CARR
DAVID CARROLL
FERGUS J. CARROLL
GLENN CARTER
RICHARD A. CARTER
JOHN E. CASHLEY
JOSEPH J. CASSIDY, JR.
CALDWELL M. CAUTHEN, JR.
JOSEPH CAVAROCCHI
ROBERT J. CHAMBERS
WILLIAM CHAPMAN, JR.
JOSEPH T. CHATBURN
ALVIN R. CHAVOUS
ROBERT J. CAMPBELL
RONALD J. CAMPBELL
KENNETH N. CHEEK

RICHARD C. CHUBB
WALERIJA CHULCHATSCHINOW
JOHN J. CIMORELLI, JR.
REUBEN L. CLARK, JR.
JAMES H. CLAY
MILTON G. CLAYBORNE
TONY CLOUGH
LOUIS A. COBARRUBIO
ALBERT COBB, JR.
CHARLES M. COHEN
LOUIS G. COHEN
JOHN M. COLE
WILLIAM P. COLL
MICHAEL T. COLLINS
DAVID W. COMBER
WILLIAM T. CONLEY
RICHARD J. CONLIN
PATRICK M. CORCORAN
DAVID H. COOPER, II
VINCENT J. CONNOLLY

JOSEPH Q. CONWAY
LESLIE COOK
ALEXANDER COOPER
LEON L. CORNWELL, JR.
RORY A. COVINGTON
JAMES J. CRAFTON III
MICHAEL J. CRESCENZ
RAY O. CROPPER
JOSEPH A. CROSS
HOVEY R. CURRY
PHILIP A. D'AMICO, JR.
JOSEPH F. DALY
DEIGHTON A. DANIELLES
FRANCIS A. M. DANIELS
DAVID L. DANOWSKI
CHARLES W. DAUT
JOSEPH E. DAVIS, JR.
EDWARD S. DAY

THOMAS J. DEAN, III
CHARLES E. DIAMOND
VICTOR DI CAVALLUCCI
DIETER W. DIETZ
WAYNE T. DILLMAN
RONALD M. DI STEFANO
STEPHEN D. DIXON
HAROLD A. DOMAN
JOHN J. DONNELLY, III
DENNIS G. DONOVAN
MICHAEL L. DORN
THEODORE A. DOUGHERTY
THOMAS J. DOWD
MICHAEL W. DOYLE
VESTIE T. DRIGGERS
STANLEY W. DRIZA
THOMAS A. DUCKETT
ROBERT J. DUPELL, JR.
RICHARD DeMARCO

WILLIE DURANT
PATRICK P. DWYER
CHARLES E. DYSON, JR.
MICHAEL L. EBALD
LEROY ELLIOTT
HUGH W. ELMORE
RUBEN ENGLISH
LARRY D. EPSTINE
CHARLES J. ESBENSEN
DONALD J. EVANS
GORDON E. EVANS
EDMUND G. EXUM, JR.
ANTHONY J. FAMILIARE
NEVIN O. FARNSWORTH, III
HERBERT L. FARRINGTON, III
JOHN R. FEESER
WALTER FELTON
ROBERT F. FERGUSON
RICHARD

WILLIAM T. FINDLAY
THEODORE E. FISCHER
THOMAS F. FLAHIVE
JOHN J. FLOOD, JR.
DAVID FLORES
TONY C. FOSTER
JERRY M. FOY
WILLIAM J. FRANKS
LORRENCE T. FRIDAY
BRUCE E. FUNK
JAMES F. GALATI
DANIEL P. GALLAGHER
JOHN J. GALLAGHER
JOSEPH T. GALLAGHER
RICHARD GALLAGHER
SAMUEL CALLMAN, III
ANTONIO GARCIA
DENNIS GARLAND
WALTER J. GARSTKIEWI

THOMAS GARTLAND
VINCENT F. GARVEY
AUSTIN M. GAUGHAN
MICHAEL A. GIANNINI
CHARLES J. GIBILTERRA, JR.
WILBERT L. GILLESPIE
RICHARD A. GILLIAM
WILLIAM D. GILLINGHAM
HAROLD T. GILLIS
CHARLES L. GLENN, III
DONALD E. GLICKMAN
ROSCOE GLOVER, JR.
CLARENCE GOBER, JR.
WALTER H. GOLASZEWSKI
DONNELL GOODMAN
HENRY W. GORMAN
LINWOOD GOUGH
JOSEPH G. DEL
CLEMENT GRASSO

## Vietnam Veterans Memorial
## "It is Our Duty to Remember"

Inspired by the Washington, D.C. Memorial, the names of 646 brave Philadelphia soldiers who served in Vietnam and lost their lives are engraved on two curved granite walls. You'll also see ten panels, eight of which are etched with war scenes. The memorial is on the corner of Front and Spruce Streets and is a beautiful place to honor these soldiers who fought our nation's longest war.

### Villanova University
### Go Wild!

This may be the oldest and largest Catholic university in Pennsylvania, but it's got a wild side —a wildcat mascot named Will D. Cat! In fact, Villanova once paraded a live bobcat named Count Villan in front of audiences at football and basketball games, but decided in 1950 to use a person dressed in a cat costume instead. Much safer! Villanova was started in 1842, has more than 10,000 students enrolled in its 5 colleges, and is located 12 miles west of Philly.

### Walnut Street Theatre
### Circus, Circus

It's hard to believe, but the oldest English-language theatre in the U.S. started off in 1809 as the home for a traveling circus. Today, the main auditorium seats 1,052 people, all with good views of the stage. The Walnut really likes its younger audiences, because it presents laugh-out-loud plays and musicals based on the antics of characters Junie B. Jones, Flat Stanley, and even the animals in *Click, Clack, Moo.*

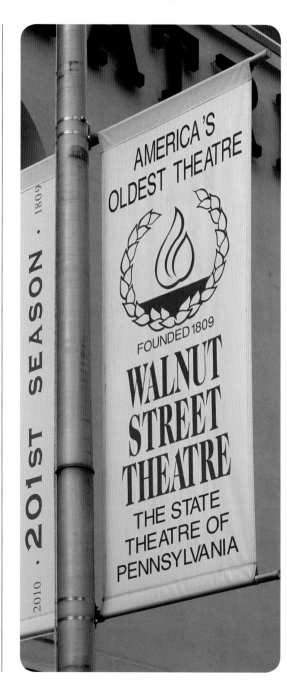

## Waterfront Park

The Camden, New Jersey, riverfront is right across from Penn's Landing and offers lots of great activities. Jump aboard a River-Link Ferry to get there and then be sure to visit the Camden Children's Garden, tour the decorated battleship USS *New Jersey*, attend a baseball game of the Camden Riversharks, listen to a concert at Wiggins Waterfront Park, or visit Adventure Aquarium.

## Water Ice: Cool Philly Treat

Water ice, or as people in Philly call it, "wudder ice," is a frozen dessert made from concentrated syrup flavoring with chunks of fresh fruit. The Chinese actually made the very first flavored water ice in 3000 B.C., but Rita's Italian Ice in Philadelphia has spread this famous treat nationwide. In 1984, Rita's founder Bob Tumolo opened his first store in Bensalem, naming the business after his wife, Rita. Bob and his mother, Elizabeth, set to work—making their product fresh daily and adding chunks of fresh fruit to the recipe. The Italian Ice was a huge hit with Philadelphians. Since then, Rita's Italian Ice has grown to over 560 locations in 18 states.

## Water Works at Fairmount Park
### Get Pumped!

These Greek Revival structures were built in 1815 as the country's first steam-pumping station. The station closed in 1909, and today, families can visit the Fairmount Water Works Interpretive Center and learn about watersheds in all kinds of exciting, unique ways. You can even fly a helicopter simulation from Delaware Bay to the headwaters of the Schuylkill River. Or visit America's most disgusting town, Pollutionopolis, to see how you can really mess up a city water supply. You can easily find this building because it is behind the Museum of Art on the Schuylkill River.

## Wave Forms
### Let Freedom Ring!

This unique and monster monument called *Wave Forms* was created by Dennis Oppenheim in 2006. Doesn't the shape of the forms remind you of something? They were designed to look like the Liberty Bell and symbolize the amazing impact it has had on Philly and its visitors. Not only can you get up close to these see-through structures, but you can walk in and around them, as well. Find them on the campus of the University of Pennsylvania.

## Wells Fargo Center
### Everything Sports—and More

Do you like pro hockey, basketball, or arena football? How about wrestling, bull riding, or concerts? You can catch them all at the Wells Fargo Center, a huge sports arena that holds more than 16,000 fans. Before a game or show, be sure to get your picture taken next to 76ers star, Julius Erving.

## William Penn
## From Prisoner to Philly Founder

It's hard to believe that someone could be thrown into jail because of his or her religious beliefs, but that is just what happened to William Penn when he lived in England. Despite all this, in 1861 Penn was given a large piece of land in the colonies where he established a colony of religious toleration, which he would call Pennsylvania. The next year, William Penn founded Philadelphia. The Founding Father—also affectionately known as Billy—was way ahead of his time. He laid out all the streets in a simple pattern that included five public squares, making Philadelphia the first "planned city" in North America.

## Wyeths
## A Painting Family

There are three generations of talented Wyeth artists. Growing up just 30 miles south of Philly in Chadds Ford, father N.C. illustrated classic children's books like *Treasure Island, Kidnapped*, and *Robinson Crusoe.* His son Andrew painted the masterpiece, *Christina's World*, among others, and grandson Jamie has illustrated two children's books and created portraits including the three Kennedy brothers, as well as still life paintings and landscapes. Visit the Brandywine River Museum in Chadds Ford, to tour the family house, as well as works from all three artists.

## X Braces on Ben Franklin Bridge
## X-tra Strong!

Famous builder Ralph Modjeski had never designed a suspension bridge before, but his Ben Franklin Bridge became known as the "first distinctly modern suspension bridge built on a grand scale." One important thing he did was add X braces, or crossbars, on the two 385-foot-high steel towers to make them strong in high winds.

## XPoNential Music Festival
### Crazy Fun Kids Corner

There's way more than music to enjoy at this annual summer festival at the Camden Waterfront. You can explore over four acres of fun on the weekend at the Kids Corner Garden, take in nature shows, go on rides, see exhibits, or bop to the beat of bands performing nonstop on the Kids Corner Garden Stage. Grab a blanket and your family and go to this bass-thumping, jumping event!

went to:
http://www.phawker.com/2010/07/19/concert-review-xponential-music-festival/#more-20604

to request permission. May have to replace if we don't get an answer.

## Yellow Mustard, Philly Style
### We're Talkin' Pretzels!

Yellow mustard on a pretzel? Are you kidding me!? Well, that's about the only way to eat a soft pretzel from Philadelphia. But do you want to know how to really enjoy a soft pretzel? Don't just buy the very first one you see. Search out the vendor who has soft, chewy pretzels that are a perfect golden brown. And be sure they don't have too much salt on them. Then squiggle a liberal coating of yellow mustard on it! Hmmm! These treats are so popular that people eat them for breakfast, lunch, and even dinner!

## YMCA
### Something for Everyone

Where can you go to play basketball, volleyball, racquetball, fustal, soccer, learn to swim, lift weights, use exercise machines, make crafts, take dance classes, study computers, learn about healthy living, participate in international understanding programs, camp by day and overnight, and do lots of fun activities for kids and adults? "Y", the YMCA of course!

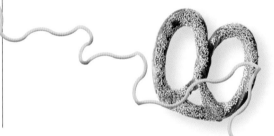

## Zoo, Philadelphia
**LEGO My Animals.**

A lot of neat stuff happens at the Philadelphia Zoo, the very first public zoo in America. You can scope out over 2000 animals of every kind, and be sure not to miss the popular Reptile and *Amphibian House* where you just might get rained on while being mesmerized by amphibians and reptiles from around the world. Or, if you dare, get up close to the lions and leopards in *Big Cat Falls*. Or float 400 feet in the air above the zoo in the Channel 6 Zooballoon. I hope you're not afraid of heights!

# Index

## My Trip to Philadelphia

**Date:**

**Stuff we did:**